# Big Red

Written by Zoë Clarke

Illustrated by Richard Watson

Broadacre Primary School

**RISING★STARS**

# Big Red Ed has a map.

# The Cod Bun Hut has cod buns!

# Gulls peck Ed and the map.

The top of the map rips off!

# Ed hops to the dock.

Ed gets in his red tug.

# Ed huffs and puffs in the muck.

Ed puffs and huffs up the rocks.

Big Red Ed is in luck.

# It is the Cod Bun Hut!

# Talk about the story

Ask your child these questions:

1  What did the seagulls peck?

2  What colour was Big Red Ed's tug boat?

3  Why did Big Red Ed huff and puff?

4  Why was Big Red Ed in luck?

5  What type of bun do you like to eat?

6  How are maps useful? Have you ever used a map?

Can your child retell the story using their own words?